BITCOIN IN 21 DAYS

Christopher Perceptions

CMPGFB LLC.

ISBN: 9798300332747

Cover design by: Christopher Perceptions
Printed in the United States of America

To every person interested in Bitcoin. This book is for you.

CONTENTS

PREFACE

"Bitcoin in 21 Days" is a book powered by TwentyOneSociety that is meant to stir thought, inspire research, and serve as an appetizer to the Bitcoin curious or Bitcoin interested. Bitcoin is money, Bitcoin is tech, and Bitcoin is a movement. This book is not an exhaustive deep dive into Bitcoin's complexities. The book serves as a challenge for you to read about Bitcoin once a day for 21 days, hence the book having 21 chapters. After 21 days, you will have a working understanding concerning Bitcoin. Consider this book your introduction to Bitcoin.

MONEY IS AN ILLUSION

What is something that we use everyday but may not understand? What is a good servant but a terrible master? What is chased but never truly owned? The answer is money. On God's green earth, the idea of exchange value for goods and services has been around for ages. Money is a tool that has changed form from the ancient to the digital in modern times. Let's take a moment to reflect on how one piece of paper has come to define where we move, what we study, how we can fashion our life, and many more things. Ultimately, money is a matter of trust, a social construct or a collective agreement that makes the suggested, printed worth hold true. Assets like gold and silver were hailed as money in history's past due to the rarity and durability of it. As time passed, money changed from assets like gold to government backed IOUs called fiat currency. Fiat currency holds no intrinsic value and is solely propped up by the governments that distribute it through vehicles such as central banks. While this made "money" more accessible, the value of money became quite diluted. At the time of this book's publishing, it would require you to hold roughly $1.45 to have the same buying power as you did 10 years ago. Many in America feel this at groceries stores, when your all bills go up $5 to $10 dollars, when you have more month than money at the end of a pay period from your 9-5. Savings, when compared to the rate of inflation, feels like a slow death to any value you may be able to hold on to. Banks often promote savings accounts with interest, but it barely scratches the surface of combating the rate of inflation while the bank makes money on your money. Inflation is known as the hidden thief of wealth and it is one of fiat currency's biggest flaws. As fiat currency is printed, its purchasing power is diminished. Central banks wield unlimited power to print and while various government entities like the Pentagon can't pass an audit to save themselves, citizens like in America are crushed under the boulder of generations of incompetence regarding monetary policy. In short, the system is broken. A black swan event, a series of bank runs, and supply chain issues would highlight what currently is the reason why America has a multi trillion dollar debt. Many governments around the world have this issue, some hide it better and some do not. Regardless, before we speak on the solution, it is important for you to have understanding of the problem.

Money as you know it is an illusion, but there is a better way.

THE GENESIS
OF BITCOIN

T he year is 2008 and America was ground zero to one of the most well known financial crises in modern history. Institutions such as Lehman Brothers collapsed, millions of Americans lost their homes, and trust in the banking system as a whole was completely broken. When the smoke cleared, there was more than Occupy Wall Street marches happening; some people took action in a way that couldn't be arrested, burned, or seized. An individual or group operating under the pseudonym "Satoshi Nakamoto" published a whitepaper entitled "Bitcoin: A Peer-to-Peer Electronic Cash System." The whitepaper presented a revolutionary idea which was a form of money that operates without middlemen, such as governments or banks, and was digital in nature while also inflation resistant. Bitcoin, in essence, is a revolutionary act as well as a direct response to the glaring failure of a greedy system that flew to close to the sun, but instead of burning, was bailed out. Regarding the people who lost their homes, they didn't receive the same treatment. They say"Gold is God's money, fiat is the government's money, and Bitcoin is the people's money." The reason for this saying is due to the simple yet profound vision that Satoshi expressed: Operate on a decentralized network where no signal entity could control it. The only thing that is relied on is a transparent, immutable ledger that records every transaction and is audited every 10 to 20 minutes on a global scale. Bitcoin aimed to be a globally fair system as well as a reliable store of value, unlike the fiat currencies that we chase. By January 2009, the first block of the Bitcoin blockchain, known as the genesis block, was mined and thus sparked a new era of freedom.

HOW BITCOIN WORKS

Bitcoin is digital money, but what makes it special is the way that it operates. Traditional systems rely on banks to keep a ledger, or record, of transactions and balances. For example, sending $100 to a person will be recorded by the bank as it updates its records to reflect the transfer. With Bitcoin, no central entities is involved. Bitcoin is a operated by a global network of computers, called nodes and they work together to maintain the Bitcoin ledger. The ledger is the blockchain, which is a series of blocks that record every Bitcoin transaction ever made, which creates enduring transparency and security. In the Bitcoin industry, the phrase is "Don't trust, verify." Due to the nature of the Bitcoin blockchain, trust assumptions are removed. You have to "trust" your bank to be able to give you your money when you want it. If you had an account with $50,000,000 in it and attempted to pull $250,000 out in cash, you would realized that you don't have control of your money; the bank simply gives you permission to get money from an account that they have control over but you have access to. Bitcoin is on the opposite side of the spectrum where blocks of data that are secure like in a chain, hence blockchain, allow for you to have complete oversight and ownership of your value at any time you want. Bitcoin gives you freedom while banks give you permission. The Bitcoin blockchain operates through a system called "Proof of Work" where miners, global operators of specialized machines, solve complex computational problems to secure validate transactions and add them to the ledger. The process makes Bitcoin decentralized and resistant to tampering as no single person or institution can alter the blockchain. Once a Bitcoin transaction is added, it is permanent. Bitcoin is used to send and receive value globally with low fees and no intermediaries. Buying a cup of coffee or transferring money across oceans? Bitcoin operates exactly the same. By design, Bitcoin is inclusive, making it a game changer for the world, especially people without access to banking systems.

POWER IN SCARCITY

Scarcity matters. When something is scarce, it is rare. Rarity promotes a sense of exclusivity and value. Gold, diamonds, and high art are examples of value in scarcity. Here's a fact regarding exclusivity: there are only 21 million Bitcoin in existence. This means that no central bank or governmental agency can say "Hey, let's do quantitative easing and create more Bitcoin out of thin air." There are more millionaires on the planet than Bitcoin which means every millionaire cannot hold one Bitcoin. This is why Bitcoin is called "digital gold." On the flip side regarding inclusivity, 1 Bitcoin is made up of 100,000,000 smaller units called Satoshis or sats for short; this is equivalent of 100 pennies to 1 dollar. While many may not ever be able to have 1 Bitcoin, anyone can currently acquire fractions of a Bitcoin. Compared to fiat currency, they are far from scarce. during the COVID-19 pandemic, governments around the world printed trillions of dollars to support their economies, causing inflation to soar. Bitcoin has no central authority that can inflate its supply of 21 million Bitcoin. As demand for Bitcoin continues to grow, its limited supply ensures it may become more valuable over time, providing a reliable hedge against economic uncertainty. Thus, saving in fiat is a losing battle while saving in Bitcoin is a matter of game theory and economics. Experts expect for 1 Bitcoin to be worth $1,000,000 by 2030 and this is the reason why.

BITCOIN VS. FIAT

Y ou can spend fiat currency and you can spend Bitcoin. You can save fiat currency and you can save Bitcoin. You can earn fiat currency and you can earn Bitcoin. While fiat currency and Bitcoin are both considered mediums of value, the differences are quite stark. Dollars, Euros, Francs, Rands, and other fiat currencies are controlled by their issued governing nations. The intrinsic value they "hold" is based on a matter of trust that the issuing governing body has, which can flutter between military might or resources or policies or figureheads in position. When you look at Bitcoin, there are a myriad of advantages. IT's more secure, it's portable, it divisible, it's inflation resistant, and it has a fixed supply. Based on this alone, Bitcoin is far superior to the current global monetary system.

PROTECT YOUR WEALTH

The world has become extremely uncertain in many respects, especially when you look at the rise of inflation eroding aware savings coupled with wars and rumors of wars causing market downturns due to possible economic instability. The system is massive as it is rigid and fragile. As we have touched on, Bitcoin's fixed supply of 21,000,000 Bitcoin ensures that the supply never changes or face debasement, making Bitcoin a solid store of value for long term holding. Bitcoin is likened to digital gold due to scarcity and its digital nature. As long as you have internet or even a mesh network, you are able to transact within the global network of the decentralized asset known as Bitcoin. Along with this,

Bitcoin is also a great hedge against economic abnormalities. When traditional markets rallied around the Game Stop stock, traders were barred out and companies like Robinhood stopped people from trading. No one can stop Bitcoin, which means no one can stop you from doing what you want to do with your Bitcoin. In a hyperinflation environment, Bitcoin is a safe haven for people looking to protect assets, buying power, liquidity, and savings.

THE SMEAR CAMPAIGN

My generation has a saying: "Haters gonna hate." While Bitcoin is skyrocketing in popularity, utility, and global acceptance, a few bad apples with influence are vocal about their skepticism. This is called FUD, which means Fear, Uncertainty, and Doubt. Many times, people shake their fist at Bitcoin due to realizing that they can't control it. The narrative of Bitcoin being used by hackers and criminals doesn't land either, because criminals do more money laundering through traditional methods than through a global, tamper proof network that has a digital ledger; for most criminals, they prefer cash or high art.

EARLY ADOPTION

Bitcoin is a prime example of the saying "slowly, then suddenly." In the Holy Bible, Zechariah 4:10 tells us not to despise the day of small beginnings. Bitcoin was accepted by a small group of forward thinking developers, cryptographers, and adopted by people who saw its potential as a tool to upend the global financial system. It's one thing for us to know that Bitcoin can be used to purchase goods and services, but how did the first transaction take place? In 2010, a programmer named Laszlo Hanvecz made Bitcoin history when he purchase two Papa John's pizzas for the modest total of 10,000 Bitcoin. It was a peer-to-peer transaction where someone used dollars to purchase the pizza then Laszlo sent Bitcoin to the person. What was modest in value back then is worth billions now. While Bitcoin Pizza Day became a holiday in the Bitcoin community to be a hallmark of the first real world transaction of Bitcoin, other outfits adopted Bitcoin also. A dark web marketplace called Silk Road used Bitcoin as the preferred method of payment and many illegal things were able to facilitate due to the unique nature of Bitcoin in being pseudo anonymous. Can you guess which of the two caused a blemish on Bitcoin in the eyes of governments? Bitcoin travailed through years of criticism where headlines said Bitcoin is dead or Bitcoin is only for criminals, etc. Many thought Bitcoin was a fad or a bubble as "magic internet money" could not really catch fire. Now, here we have the world studying Bitcoin. How things have changed.

MINE YOUR BUSINESS

We are going to dive into a technical topic, but I promise that I won't veer off too deep. Bitcoin mining is misunderstood yet deeply essential because mining along side running a Bitcoin node are the anchor blocks to how this decentralized network operation on a global scale. Miners are people or entities that use specialized, powerful computers to solve cryptographic equations to validate transactions and secure Bitcoin. That's a mouthful, right? Basically, miners are doing audits on Bitcoin using special computers. Anyone with the capital to setup a mining operation can mine and be among the "auditors" of Bitcoin. Satoshi Nakamoto even built in a reward mechanism where if a Bitcoin block is mined by you, you earn Bitcoin and transaction fees as a reward! This process is called "proof of work". Miners technically spend money to have electricity to mine Bitcoin. Back in the day, you could mine hundreds of Bitcoin from your personal computer, but as the network grew, requirements increased. Miners use ASICs, which is short for Application-Specific Integrated Circuits, to compete for rewards. Miners are the unsung heroes of Bitcoin.

EXCHANGE EVOLUTION

While miners spend money to buy electricity to mine Bitcoin, most people exchange money for Bitcoin. With Bitcoin gaining traction, marketplaces known as Bitcoin exchanges became a huge need for adoption to grow. With exchanges like Mt. Gox, an economy began to emerge, until a shaking took place. Mt. Gox was hacked and lost over 700,000 Bitcoin. Despite the challenges, better exchanges were born from the fire. Major exchanges such as Coinbase, Finance, Kraken, Gemini, OKX and more emerged. Security, regulatory compliance, accessibility, and products for novice as well as advanced traders came to the forefront, making it easy for anyone to make their first Bitcoin purchase. Exchanges took Bitcoin from a niche asset used by the few to global phenomenon desired by the many.

PLATFORM OF PRODUCTION

Many people are unaware that Bitcoin is software that can be built upon. The exploration that many people know exists within other blockchains originally wanted to live on Bitcoin. Now, it is possible through L2s, which is short for Layer 2s. Bitcoin can be built on using a programming language called Bitscript as well as Miniscript. The language is rigid and limited, so many people look to L2s such as Stacks, Rootstock, or even L2s that have a form of Bitcoin on them such as Base, from the exchange Coinbase, to build decentralized apps that are censorship resistant. L2s extend Bitcoin's functionality while preserving the integrity of the Bitcoin network. Many believe that L2s will usher in an era of building on Bitcoin as well as unlock the Bitcoin economy for mass adoption.

INCUBATION FOR INCLUSION

There is a growing use case for Bitcoin which is its ability to cultivate financial inclusion for the underbanked and unbanked populations of the world, which is over 1 billion people. People shouldn't be penalized for their skin color, where they are geographically located, what family they may have been born into, the economic setup of their household, etc. Bitcoin offers freedom through means that are normal for many of these people, a smartphone with data. This tool can unlock a world of opportunity. In places like El Salvador and South Africa, Bitcoin is empowering people to send and receive money without crazy fees or delays. Workers sending remittances are able to send Bitcoin to family and they are able to receive nearly 100% of what is sent. Bitcoin's open network allows for people born under oppressive regimes to access a globally neutral currency. This is world changing and Nobel Peace Prize worthy technology.

THE ENVIRONMENT

If electricity is used to mine Bitcoin, does that mean Bitcoin is bad for the environment? While it is true that Bitcoin requires a lot of electricity, there are a lot of things that use a significant amount of electricity which is hardly heard about. The military, fracking, drying clothes, and more use a seismic amount of electricity, but they are controlled. Bitcoin cannot be controlled, it can only be regulated. While the conspiracy against Bitcoin is real, the Bitcoin industry has adopted new methods of generating energy that are less reliant on centralized tools such as the grid of a municipality. Now, Bitcoin can be mined with renewable energy and off grind energy setups. A narrative has grown concerning grid based energy where surplus electricity is often wasted and Bitcoin miners help the grid. Nevertheless, Bitcoin doesn't like to be pigeon holed, so new operations are spinning up using hydro, wind, and solar. Traditional banking uses a lot of energy. Mining gold and the cobalt in EV batteries take a lot of energy. Bitcoin, providing a transparent alternative, allows for miners to setup renewable mining operations to help the environment, secure the Bitcoin network, and have a viable business.

GLOBAL ADOPTION

From El Salvador adopting it as legal tender to being able to pay for groceries using it in South Africa, the global impact of Bitcoin is completely and utterly undeniable. In countries with much economic instability, like Turkey and Lebanon, the adoption of Bitcoin has surged as people turn to it as a hedge against hyperinflation and governmental controls. Regions high in remittance have a high interest in Bitcoin as it is a cost-effective way to transfer money across borders. The adoption of Bitcoin isn't limited to underbanked people and unbanked people in dire situations. Family offices, institutions, hedge funds, and even a handful of governments are recognizing its potential. PayPal and Square have integrated Bitcoin into their offerings. Tesla and Microstrategy hold billions of dollars worth of Bitcoin in their corporate treasury which is creating a trend among many corporations. Some call this the "Orange Wave."

ECONOMIC LIBERTY

Humans desire freedom. We have a propensity to seek things that promise freedom, but many things rarely give us freedom. We buy a home and believe it's ours. If we don't pay property taxes, we find out who really owns the home. This is merely one example of many. Billions of people on the planet live under systems where financial freedoms are restricted or worse, nonexistent. For people living in economically unstable regions, Bitcoin is "Plan B" or the "Escape Plan". Do you know the story of the trillion dollar bill? In the early 2000s, Zimbabwe experienced one of the worst hyperinflation crises in history. Due to excessive money printing by the central bank to cover government debt and fund unsustainable governmental outputs, the value of the Zimbabwean dollar plummeted. Prices skyrocketed due to hyperinflation, and eventually, the government issued fiat currency in denominations as high as 100 trillion dollars. By 2009, the currency became worthless, and the country abandoned it in favor of foreign currencies like the US dollar. Bitcoin as decentralized money creates the opportunity for anyone to have a shot at a fair system. This is what drew me to Bitcoin, the concept of a truly fair system.

LIGHTNING SPEED

The Lightning Network is a darling among many Bitcoin enthusiast due to its speed. Bitcoin blocks are mined in 10 - 20 minute intervals, making mass adoption slightly difficult. Something can be better in theory, but if it's not able to compete, most people will stay with the status quo. This is where the Lightning Network comes into play. As the name suggests, the Lightning Network is a separate network, considered a Bitcoin L2 or a side chain by some, that interacts with Bitcoin but makes fast transactions possible with Bitcoin. It enables instant, low-cost transactions by creating off-chain payment channels between users. These channels allow multiple transactions to occur without recording each one on the main blockchain, significantly improving speed and efficiency. The Lightning Network has revolutionized Bitcoin micro-transactions and everyday payments. Along with this, it has facilitated innovative use cases, such as streaming payments and creator tipping in real time. As the Lightning Network continues to grow, it's transforming Bitcoin from a store of value to a practical medium of exchange that's able to compete with Visa. Cash App, from Square, even integrated the Lightning Network as an option.

PHILANTHROPY UNCHAINED

Have you ever tried to give money away? I'm not talking about $5, I'm talking about $50,000 and above. The rules and regulations around gifts are scrupulous. Without proper structures in place, the gift you give may become a burden on paper. Bitcoin serves as a powerful tool for philanthropy and social impact. Traditional charitable systems stall from inefficiencies, high administrative costs, and lack of transparency. Bitcoin addresses these issues by enabling direct, peer-to-peer donations that can be fast, borderless, and verifiable on the blockchain. Organizations can receive funds without intermediaries, ensuring more of the donation reaches those in need. During global crises like the COVID-19 pandemic or the conflict in Ukraine, Bitcoin has allowed individuals to provide immediate financial support to affected regions, bypassing traditional banking delays. Bitcoin philanthropy demonstrates Bitcoin's potential to transform altruistic giving in a real way.

RUSE & REGULATION

Every innovation comes with a new challenge. Apple and Steve Jobs introduced the iPhone, then a market for screen protectors and iPhone cases exploded because people didn't want their glass screen shattered or their iPhone get waterlogged while on vacation. The same applies to Bitcoin, except the challenges came from governments around the world. People often fear what they don't understand and hate what they cannot control. For example, China impose strict bans on Bitcoin. While the regulatory environment globally varies based on jurisdiction, the challenges are still just as real but the stakes are higher. Regulation that is clear and has been welcomed by the Bitcoin industry for years. One point of contention has been how to properly identify Bitcoin. Is it a currency, commodity, or security? Should it be legal tender? How does tax apply to Bitcoin, if at all? Do trades warrant taxation like real estate when it's sold since it could be perceived as property? There is a plethora of nuance with Bitcoin still. While advocacy groups are working tirelessly to educate policymakers for the benefit of society as a whole. Despite hurdles, Bitcoin shows its capacity to adapt and to be adopted.

BITCOIN DEVELOPMENT

Without Bitcoin developers, Bitcoin would not exist. From Satoshi Nakamoto to Hal Finney, Bitcoin is cultivated and sustained in an open source environment. As an open-source project, Bitcoin allows anyone to contribute to its codebase, fostering innovation and collaboration. Developers introduced enhancements and updates to ensure Bitcoin remains secure and adaptable to future challenges. Along with protocol maintenance, developers create apps, wallets, and tools that expand Bitcoin's usability. From hardware wallets like One Key to user-friendly apps like Alby, innovations make Bitcoin accessible to a wider audience. It's worth noting that being a

Bitcoin developer is not a smooth road of a career path as many developers are grant supported or do contract work. One of the most selfless things a person can do in the Bitcoin industry is be a core developer.

DECENTRALIZED FINANCE

Bitcoin as a decentralized currency has unlocked the door for decentralized finance, affectionately known as DeFi. DeFi platforms allow for users to trade, lend, borrow, and earn interest on Bitcoin without relying on credit systems or traditional banking systems. This will empower any holder of Bitcoin to leverage Bitcoin in financial activities while maintaining control over funds. DeFi thrives based on trustless or trust minimized protocols which reduce the risk of fraud or mismanagement. The versatility and potential of DeFi is to disrupt traditional finance.

THE ECONOMY
OF BITCOIN

T he only certainty is that nothing is certain. While the future of Bitcoin is promising, nothing is for sure. This is not financial advice, but merely an educational guide for you. As adoption grows, challenges like scalability and regulatory scrutiny will require innovative solutions. Technological advancements, such as sidechains and L2s, hold the potential to address these issues and unlock new possibilities for Bitcoin's use. Bitcoin's role in the global economy continues to expand. Whether as a hedge against inflation, a tool for financial inclusion, or a foundation for decentralized applications, Bitcoin's impact is undeniable. The growing interest from institutions, governments, and individuals suggests that Bitcoin is not just a passing trend but a transformative force reshaping how the world views money and value. Bitcoin has changed the world. I believe that one way or another, Bitcoin will change your life.

AFTERWORD

As you have successfully finished this 21-day journey through the world of Bitcoin, I ask that you reflect on what Bitcoin means beyond hype and headlines. Yes, Bitcoin is a digital currency, but it also is a tool of self empowerment, taking citizens from passive participants within a jurisdiction and turning this into sovereign self custodians of value. Bitcoin has not yet reached mass adoption at the time of the publishing of this book, yet it is currently a trillion dollar asset that nation states, multinational corporations, and billionaires are beginning to accumulate en mass, yet people were in Bitcoin before the three previously mentioned categories of holders. That's the power of Bitcoin, it democratizes financial freedom. What happens now is up to you. Will you dive deeper in your exploration? Will you join a Bitcoin meetup? Will you buy and hold Bitcoin as an asset? Will you earn in fiat and save in Bitcoin? Will you live off of Bitcoin?

I look forward to seeing what you do next as a member of

TwentyOneSociety! Thank you and God bless. Shalom.

ABOUT THE AUTHOR

Christopher Perceptions

 Christopher Perceptions stands at the intersection of AI, Bitcoin, and NoCode innovation, enabling Bitcoin to transcend its role as a mere currency to become the bedrock of creative development and equitable digital strategies. For nearly a decade, Christopher has been a driving force in shaping the future of decentralized technology.

Christopher's vision is centered on mass adoption. His approach democratizes Bitcoin and Layer 2 development, making it accessible and comprehensible to both enthusiasts and entrepreneurs.

Author of the bestselling book "The Secrets of Satoshi: Understanding Bitcoin," Christopher has made a global impact through education. He has enlightened thousands and has been a featured speaker at premier conferences like Bitcoin Unleashed.

Through his weekly newsletter, "Christopher's Perceptions," he offers a wealth of knowledge, making complex topics in Bitcoin, Web3, and NoCode accessible to a global audience. Christopher is more than a leader; he's a coach, guiding entrepreneurs as they navigate and succeed in the ever-evolving Web3 domain.

A bridge between technical innovation and community engagement, Christopher reinforces his belief in Bitcoin as a system embodying fairness, innovation, and interdependence, paving the way for an impactful future. Christopher is the founder of TwentyOneSociety.

BOOKS BY THIS AUTHOR

The Secrets Of Satoshi - Understanding Bitcoin

"The Secrets of Satoshi: Understanding Bitcoin" is a comprehensive guide to the world of Bitcoin. It provides clear and concise answers to the most common questions about this revolutionary digital currency. The book covers the history of Bitcoin and the concepts presented in the Bitcoin whitepaper. It also includes an overview of blockchain technology, mining, and security. Whether you're an experienced Bitcoin enthusiast or a curious beginner, The Secrets of Satoshi equips you with the knowledge you need to navigate the intricacies of Bitcoin with confidence. You'll learn about the inner workings of this decentralized payment system, its potential to disrupt finance, and its long-term implications. To truly understand Bitcoin, you must understand how it has transformed the world. Understand the secrets of Satoshi with Christopher Perceptions.

www.ingramcontent.com/pod-product-compliance
Lightning Source LLC
Chambersburg PA
CBHW070135230526
45472CB00004B/1541